HOW THE INCREDIBLE HUMAN BODY WORKS
by the Brainwaves

Illustrated by
Lisa Swerling
and Ralph Lazar

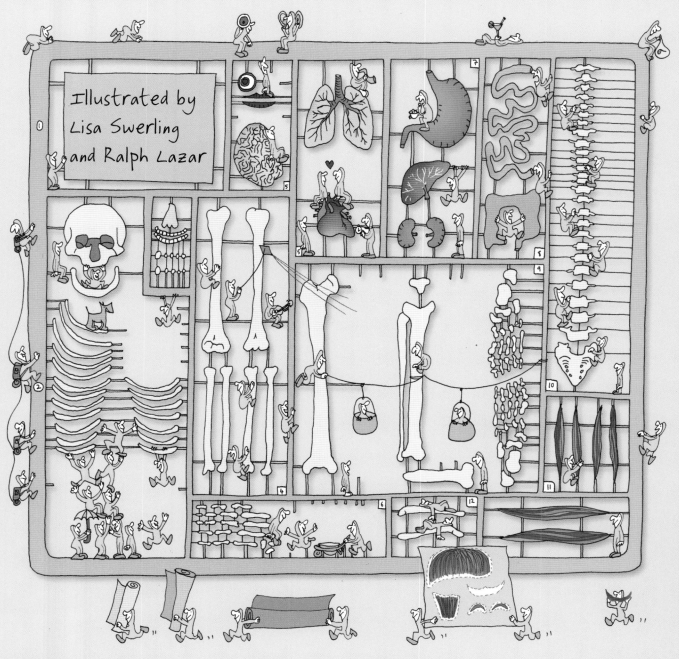

written by Richard Walker

CONTENTS

It's a really incredible book

What an amazing body!

It's super duper

Ta-da!

DK

LONDON, NEW YORK, MELBOURNE, MUNICH, and DELHI

Project Editor   Niki Foreman
Designer   Jim Green

Managing Editor   Linda Esposito
Managing Art Editor   Diane Thistlethwaite

Consultant   Dr Sue Davidson

Jacket Copywriter   Adam Powley
Jacket Editor   Mariza O'Keeffe
Indexer   Lynn Bresler

Publishing Manager   Andrew Macintyre

Category Publisher   Laura Buller

Production Controller   Angela Graef

First published in Great Britain in 2007
by Dorling Kindersley Limited,
80 Strand, London WC2R 0RL

A CIP catalogue record for this book is available from
the British Library.

ISBN: 978 1 40532 174 7

Colour reproduction by Wyndeham-Icon, UK,
and GRB Editrice s.r.l., UK

Printed and bound by Hung Hing, China

Discover more at
www.dk.com
www.thebrainwaves.com

About this book

Featuring the Brainwaves – those little people with big ideas – this fascinating book takes a light-hearted but extremely informative look at how the incredible human body works. See in minute detail all the bodily processes, and discover how they interrelate to produce the most amazing thing ever created – a human. A key feature is the six double gatefolds, each of which focuses on a key body system. There are also special features on a comprehensive range of subjects, such as communication and the basic building blocks of life.

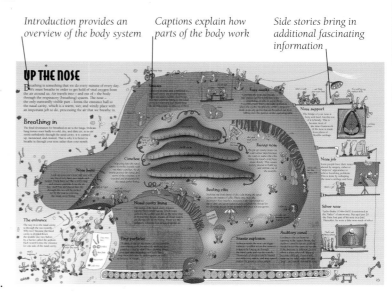

Introduction provides an overview of the body system

Captions explain how parts of the body work

Side stories bring in additional fascinating information

Introduction

The top two pages of each gatefold is where we begin our journey. Respiration begins with breathing in, and here, the nose is depicted as a giant vacuum cleaner.

Locater shows the anatomy of each body system

Many devices lead you through the scene

Pull-out magnifications provide in-depth information about important features

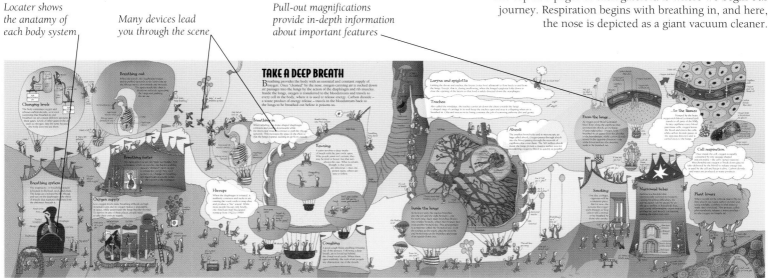

Folded-out gatefold

The gatefold folds out to reveal, in fascinating detail, the anatomy and physiology of the respiratory system and explores the connections with other body systems.

The Brainwaves have a lot to say!

Signposts direct you through the landscape

Look out for me!

Throughout the book, I'll be busy loading up my trolley and filling my brain with fantastic ideas. At the end of the book, I will create something of my very own …

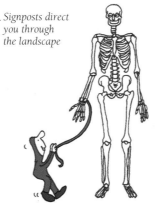

Special features

In between each of the gatefolds, we take a look at the incredible human body from a different perspective, taking a wacky view of subjects, such as how inventions might change a body of the future, and what our skins do for us.

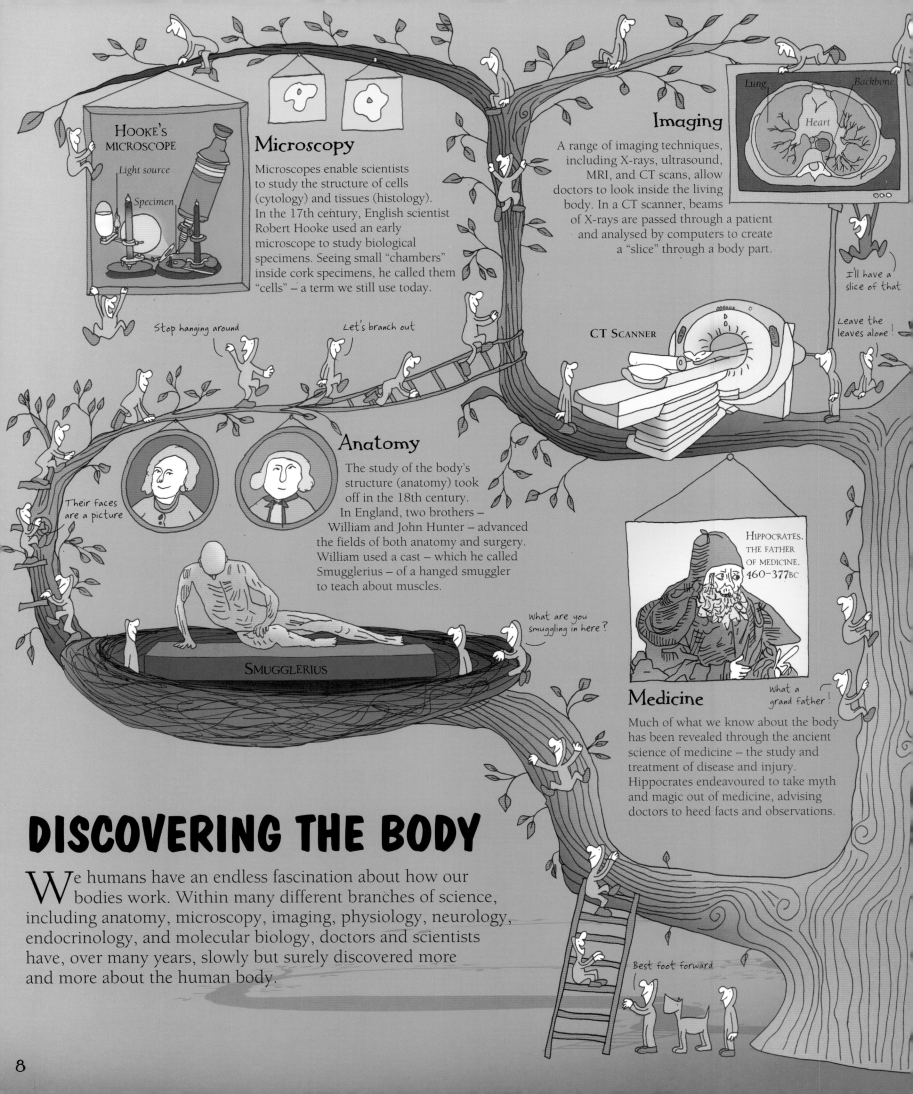

Microscopy

HOOKE'S MICROSCOPE

Light source

Specimen

Microscopes enable scientists to study the structure of cells (cytology) and tissues (histology). In the 17th century, English scientist Robert Hooke used an early microscope to study biological specimens. Seeing small "chambers" inside cork specimens, he called them "cells" – a term we still use today.

Stop hanging around

Let's branch out

Imaging

Lung *Backbone*

Heart

A range of imaging techniques, including X-rays, ultrasound, MRI, and CT scans, allow doctors to look inside the living body. In a CT scanner, beams of X-rays are passed through a patient and analysed by computers to create a "slice" through a body part.

CT SCANNER

I'll have a slice of that

Leave the leaves alone!

Anatomy

The study of the body's structure (anatomy) took off in the 18th century. In England, two brothers – William and John Hunter – advanced the fields of both anatomy and surgery. William used a cast – which he called Smugglerius – of a hanged smuggler to teach about muscles.

Their faces are a picture

SMUGGLERIUS

What are you smuggling in here?

Medicine

HIPPOCRATES. THE FATHER OF MEDICINE. 460–377BC

What a grand father!

Much of what we know about the body has been revealed through the ancient science of medicine – the study and treatment of disease and injury. Hippocrates endeavoured to take myth and magic out of medicine, advising doctors to heed facts and observations.

DISCOVERING THE BODY

We humans have an endless fascination about how our bodies work. Within many different branches of science, including anatomy, microscopy, imaging, physiology, neurology, endocrinology, and molecular biology, doctors and scientists have, over many years, slowly but surely discovered more and more about the human body.

Best foot forward

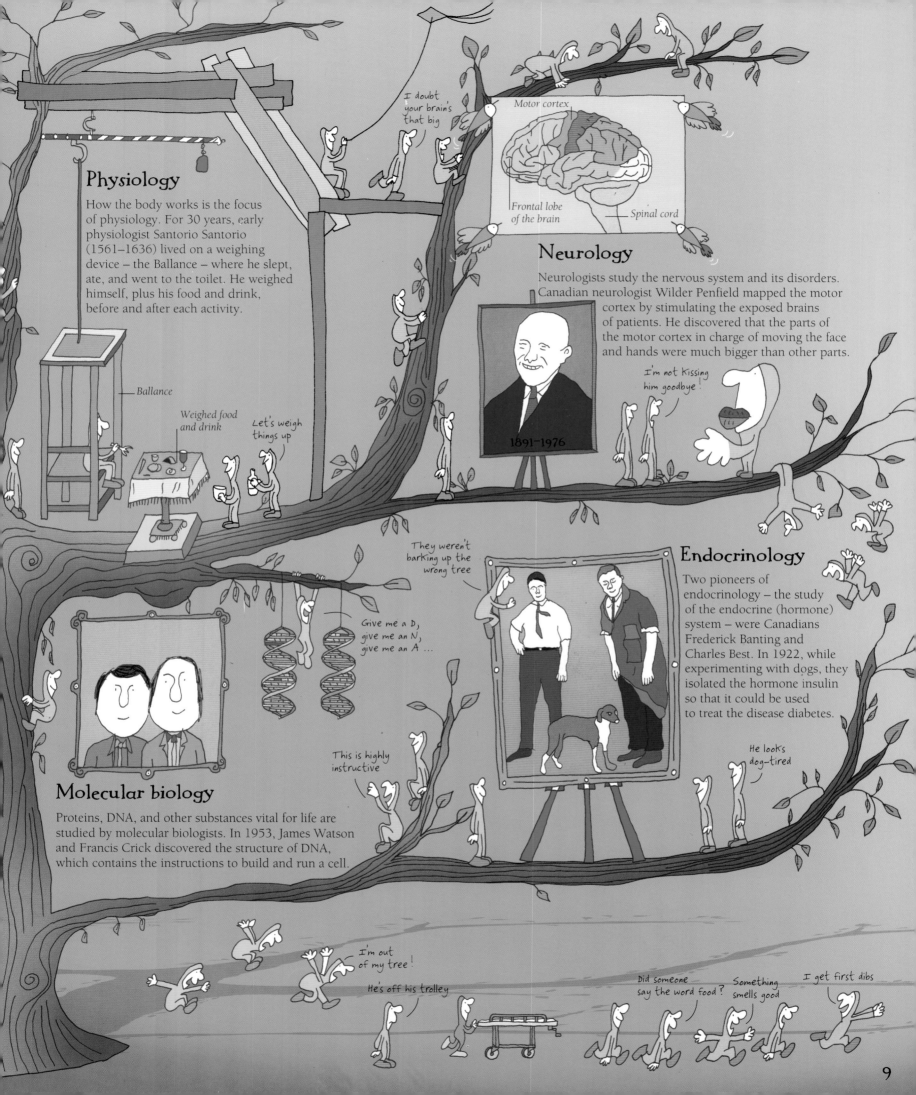

Physiology

How the body works is the focus of physiology. For 30 years, early physiologist Santorio Santorio (1561–1636) lived on a weighing device – the Ballance – where he slept, ate, and went to the toilet. He weighed himself, plus his food and drink, before and after each activity.

— Ballance

Weighed food and drink

Let's weigh things up

I doubt your brain's that big

Motor cortex

Frontal lobe of the brain — Spinal cord

Neurology

Neurologists study the nervous system and its disorders. Canadian neurologist Wilder Penfield mapped the motor cortex by stimulating the exposed brains of patients. He discovered that the parts of the motor cortex in charge of moving the face and hands were much bigger than other parts.

1891–1976

I'm not kissing him goodbye!

Molecular biology

Proteins, DNA, and other substances vital for life are studied by molecular biologists. In 1953, James Watson and Francis Crick discovered the structure of DNA, which contains the instructions to build and run a cell.

They weren't barking up the wrong tree

Give me a D, give me an N, give me an A ...

This is highly instructive

Endocrinology

Two pioneers of endocrinology – the study of the endocrine (hormone) system – were Canadians Frederick Banting and Charles Best. In 1922, while experimenting with dogs, they isolated the hormone insulin so that it could be used to treat the disease diabetes.

He looks dog-tired

I'm out of my tree!

He's off his trolley

Did someone say the word food?

Something smells good

I get first dibs

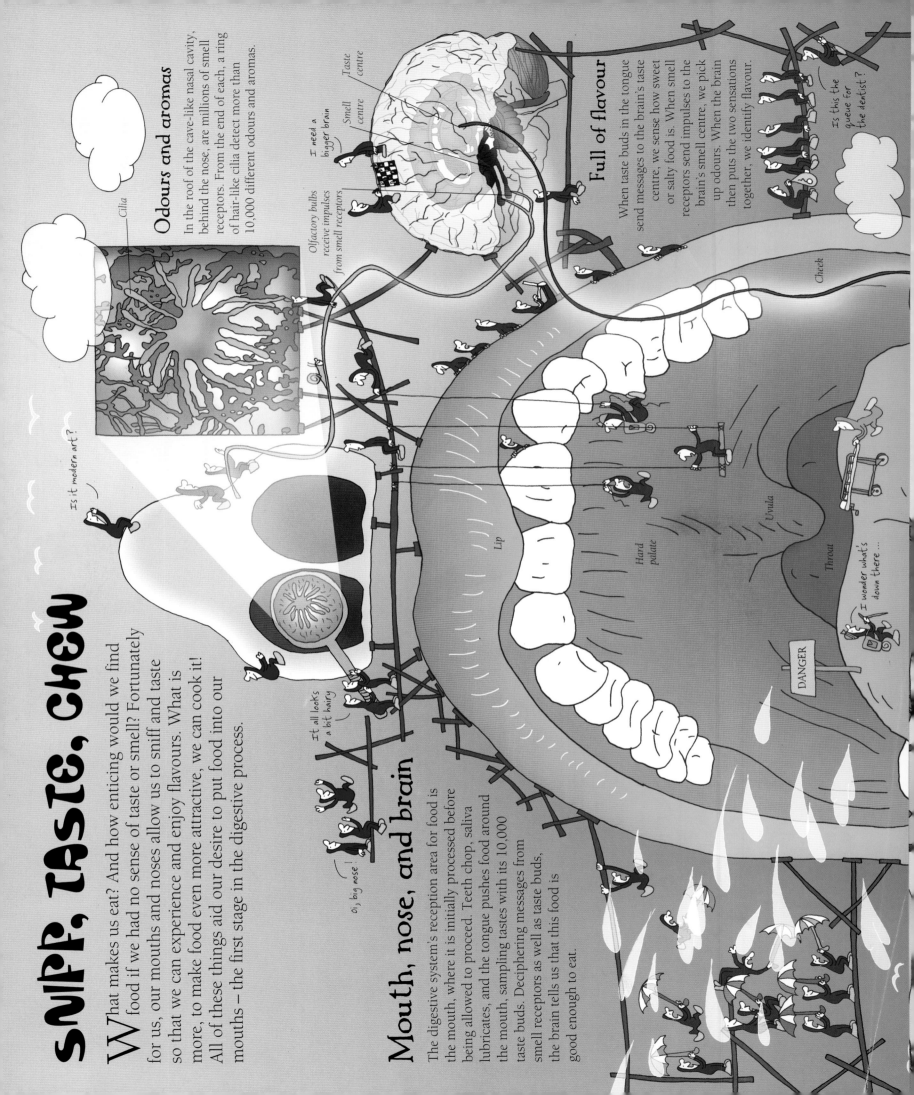

SNIFF, TASTE, CHEW

What makes us eat? And how enticing would we find food if we had no sense of taste or smell? Fortunately for us, our mouths and noses allow us to sniff and taste so that we can experience and enjoy flavours. What is more, to make food even more attractive, we can cook it! All of these things aid our desire to put food into our mouths — the first stage in the digestive process.

Odours and aromas

In the roof of the cave-like nasal cavity, behind the nose, are millions of smell receptors. From the end of each, a ring of hair-like cilia detect more than 10,000 different odours and aromas.

Mouth, nose, and brain

The digestive system's reception area for food is the mouth, where it is initially processed before being allowed to proceed. Teeth chop, saliva lubricates, and the tongue pushes food around the mouth, sampling tastes with its 10,000 taste buds. Deciphering messages from smell receptors as well as taste buds, the brain tells us that this food is good enough to eat.

Full of flavour

When taste buds in the tongue send messages to the brain's taste centre, we sense how sweet or salty food is. When smell receptors send impulses to the brain's smell centre, we pick up odours. When the brain then puts the two sensations together, we identify flavour.

Cilia

Smell centre

Taste centre

I need a bigger brain

Olfactory bulbs receive impulses from smell receptors

Is it modern art?

It all looks a bit hairy

Oi, big nose!

Lip

Hard palate

Uvula

Cheek

Throat

DANGER

I wonder what's down there ...

Is this the queue for the dentist?

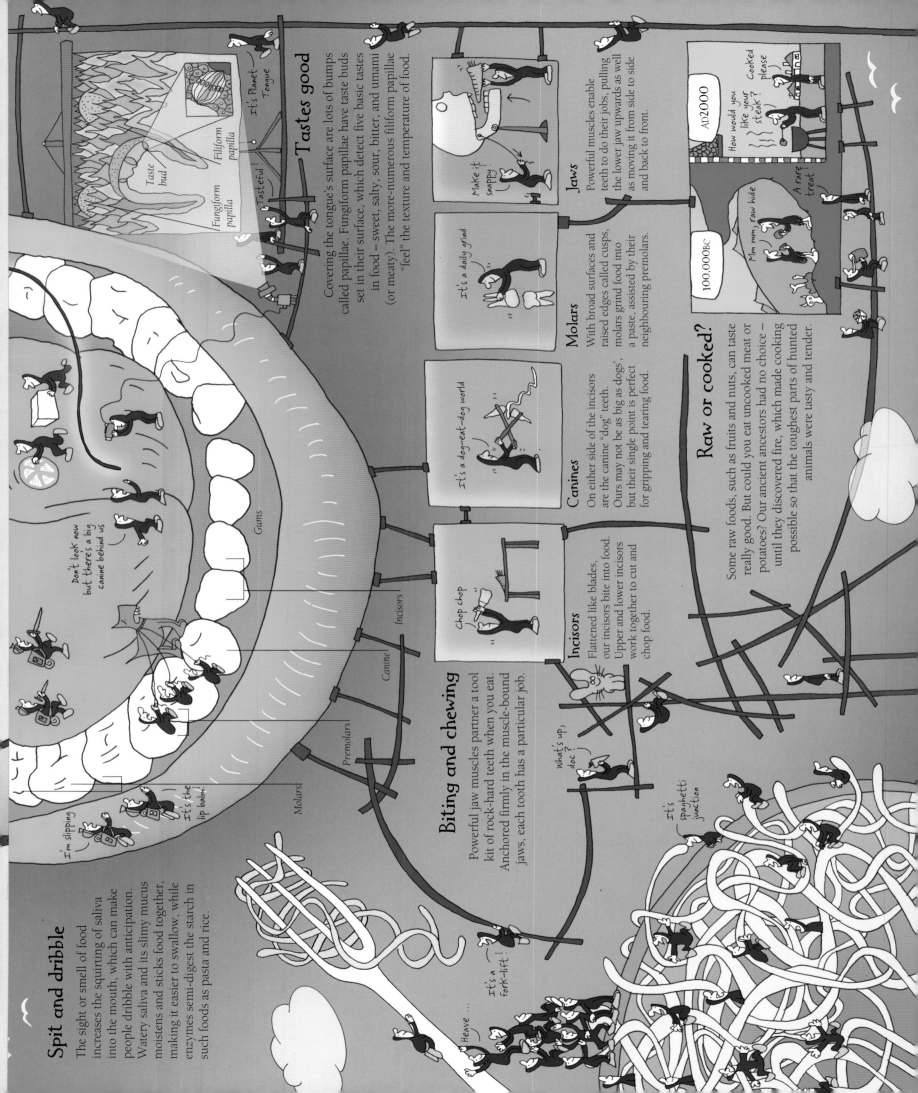

Spit and dribble

The sight or smell of food increases the squirting of saliva into the mouth, which can make people dribble with anticipation. Watery saliva and its slimy mucus moistens and sticks food together, making it easier to swallow, while enzymes semi-digest the starch in such foods as pasta and rice.

Tastes good

Covering the tongue's surface are lots of bumps called papillae. Fungiform papillae have taste buds set in their surface, which detect five basic tastes in food – sweet, salty, sour, bitter, and umami (or meaty). The more-numerous filiform papillae "feel" the texture and temperature of food.

Biting and chewing

Powerful jaw muscles partner a tool kit of rock-hard teeth when you eat. Anchored firmly in the muscle-bound jaws, each tooth has a particular job.

Incisors

Flattened like blades, our incisors bite into food. Upper and lower incisors work together to cut and chop food.

Canines

On either side of the incisors are the canine "dog" teeth. Ours may not be as big as dogs', but their single point is perfect for gripping and tearing food.

Molars

With broad surfaces and raised edges called cusps, molars grind food into a paste, assisted by their neighbouring premolars.

Jaws

Powerful muscles enable teeth to do their jobs, pulling the lower jaw upwards as well as moving it from side to side and back to front.

Raw or cooked?

Some raw foods, such as fruits and nuts, can taste really good. But could you eat uncooked meat or potatoes? Our ancient ancestors had no choice – until they discovered fire, which made cooking possible so that the toughest parts of hunted animals were tasty and tender.

RECIPE FOR LIFE

We all start life as a single cell – a fertilized egg. This basic unit of life divides repeatedly to produce a human body made of one hundred trillion cells. These cells are not identical – there are more than 200 different types, each with its own job, including fat, nerve, and bone cells. Each cell contains the genes (instructions) to construct and run not just a cell, but also an entire body.

Cell ingredients

Nucleus (containing a nucleolus, where ribosomes are made)

Cytoplasm containing:
Mitochondria
Rough endoplasmic reticulum
Golgi body
Ribosomes

Cell membrane (the outer coating)

Chromosomes and DNA

Inside each nucleus are 46 gene-carrying chromosomes made of DNA – a long molecule of two strands that spiral round each other like a twisted ladder. The rungs of this ladder, called bases, form coded instructions for making proteins, which construct and run the cell.

Ribosome makes proteins

Rough endoplasmic reticulum (ER) transports the proteins made by the ribosome

Golgi body packages the proteins made by the ribosome

Mitochondrion provides the cell with energy

Cytoplasm

Quick, let's make a shopping list

Nucleus

Cell membrane

Cell structure

Whatever their shape and size, all cells share the same basic structure. Each has an outer cell membrane, a nucleus (the control centre), and a jelly-like cytoplasm containing tiny organelles that bring the cell to life, including ribosomes, rough ER, the Golgi body, and mitochondria.

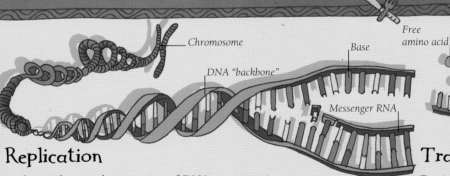

Chromosome

DNA "backbone"

Base

Messenger RNA

Free amino acid

Ribosome

Linked amino acids form a protein

Messenger RNA

Replication

In the nucleus, a short section of DNA, representing a single gene (instruction), "unzips" to expose its coded message. This is copied onto a single-stranded substance, similar to the DNA "backbone", called messenger RNA. The messenger RNA then passes out of the nucleus into the cell's cytoplasm.

Translation

Passing through a ribosome in the cytoplasm, the RNA "message" is translated into a specific sequence for free amino acids in the cytoplasm to link up correctly and form a protein.

Folding up

The new protein now detaches itself from the ribosome and folds up into its specific shape, determined by the order of amino acids.

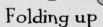

Put a lid on it

I'm nervous

Fat cells

The space inside these cells is mainly occupied by a globule of fat. Fat cells make adipose tissue, which provides an energy store and insulates the body.

Nerve cells

Nerve cells provide the wiring for the nervous system. Connected together in a massive network, they transmit electrical signals at high speed.

Bone cells

Bone cells live in isolation of each other, surrounded by the hard material that makes up bones, but still communicate to maintain bone tissue.

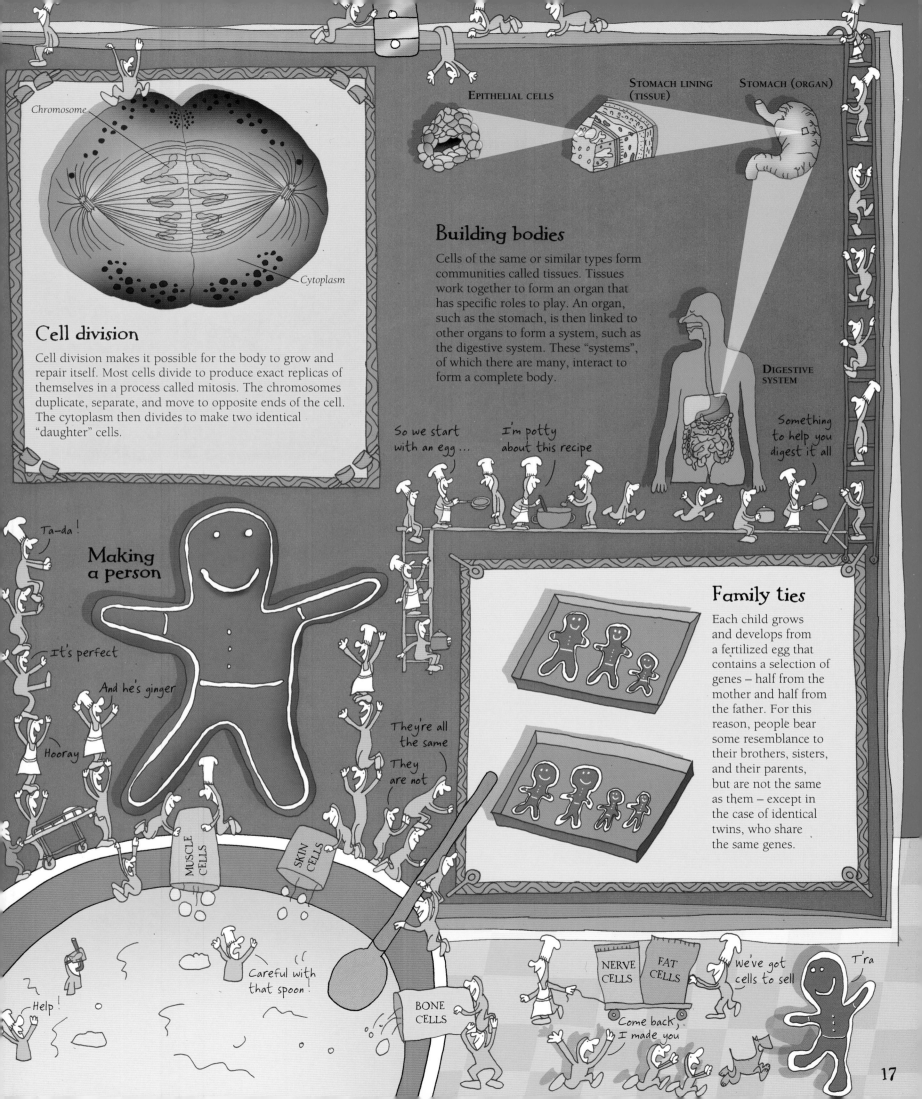

Chromosome

Cytoplasm

Cell division

Cell division makes it possible for the body to grow and repair itself. Most cells divide to produce exact replicas of themselves in a process called mitosis. The chromosomes duplicate, separate, and move to opposite ends of the cell. The cytoplasm then divides to make two identical "daughter" cells.

EPITHELIAL CELLS

STOMACH LINING (TISSUE)

STOMACH (ORGAN)

Building bodies

Cells of the same or similar types form communities called tissues. Tissues work together to form an organ that has specific roles to play. An organ, such as the stomach, is then linked to other organs to form a system, such as the digestive system. These "systems", of which there are many, interact to form a complete body.

DIGESTIVE SYSTEM

So we start with an egg …

I'm potty about this recipe

Something to help you digest it all

Making a person

Ta-da!

It's perfect

And he's ginger

Hooray

They're all the same

They are not

MUSCLE CELLS

SKIN CELLS

Careful with that spoon!

Help!

BONE CELLS

NERVE CELLS

FAT CELLS

We've got cells to sell

Come back, I made you

T'ra

Family ties

Each child grows and develops from a fertilized egg that contains a selection of genes – half from the mother and half from the father. For this reason, people bear some resemblance to their brothers, sisters, and their parents, but are not the same as them – except in the case of identical twins, who share the same genes.

UP THE NOSE

Breathing is something that we do every minute of every day. We must breathe in order to get hold of vital oxygen from the air around us. Air travels into – and out of – the body through the respiratory (breathing) system. The nose – the only outwardly visible part – forms the entrance hall to the nasal cavity, which is a warm, wet, and windy place with an important job to do, processing the air that we breathe in.

Breathing in

The final destination for breathed-in air is the lungs. Delicate lung tissues react badly to cold, dry, and dirty air, so as air swirls turbulently through the nasal cavity, it is warmed up, moistened, and cleaned. That is why it is better to breathe in through your nose rather than your mouth.

Nose hairs

Look up someone's nose and you will see lots of tiny hairs just inside each nostril. These hairs act like a net to trap and remove particles from the air. Any small bits and pieces that slip through this net will be picked up by the mucus covering the nasal cavity lining.

The entrance

The way in to the nasal cavity is through the two nostrils. Why two? Because the nasal cavity is divided down the middle into two halves by a barrier called the septum. Each nostril forms the entrance for one side of the nasal cavity.

Sinuses

Clustered around, and connected to, the nasal cavity are several sinuses. These are spaces within skull bones that have a similar lining to the nasal cavity for warming and moistening the air that passes in and out of them.

Conchae

Projecting into the nasal cavity from the outside wall are three conchae. As air swirls around the twists and turns of the conchae, it is warmed and moistened by the nasal cavity lining.

Nasal cavity lining

The lining of the nasal cavity releases a sticky fluid called mucus, which traps particles like pollen and dirt at the same time as moistening the air. Masses of blood vessels are also present in the lining. These act like radiators, releasing heat to warm up the air.

Tiny particles

Floating in the air are masses of tiny particles just waiting to be breathed in. Most are dust particles – that is, skin flakes, clothing fibres, plus dust mite droppings and body bits. And there may also be pollen grains, as well as bacteria or viruses.

Beep beep

Sinus

Boo!

Upper concha

I must have got up his nose!

Middle concha

Lower concha

This is snot funny!

Mucus

Hold on tight

Don't let anything through!

Nostril

Cilia

Dust mite bits

Pollen

Skin flake

Bacterium

Cold virus

We're gone with the wind

What's happening?

Who knows?

Nose dive!

Face masks

Covering the nose and mouth,
face masks can have different roles
depending on who is using them.
A cyclist's mask filters out traffic pollution
when the cyclist breathes in, while a surgeon's
mask stops any germs that are breathed out from
falling onto the patient on the operating table.

Nose support

The bridge of your nose is
bony and hard, but the rest
of it is bendy. This is
because most of
the inner framework
of the nose is made
from plates of
flexible cartilage.

Cartilage plates

Face muscle

Runny nose

People get runny noses on
cold winter days because
the cold air makes the cilia
lining the nasal cavity beat
more slowly. This causes
watery mucus to build up
and dribble out of
the nostrils.

Cilia

Nose job

Some people have their noses
altered by surgery, either to
"improve" appearance or
relieve breathing problems.
This is done by reshaping
the nose's cartilage and bone.

Beating cilia

Sticking out from many of the cells lining the nasal
cavity are masses of cilia. These tiny, hair-like
structures beat together, swaying from side to side to
move dirt- and germ-laden mucus towards the throat for
swallowing. Juices in the stomach will then kill any germs.

Silver nose

Tycho Brahe (1546–1601) is renowned as
the "father" of astronomy. But aged just 20,
the Dane lost part of his nose in a duel.
Thereafter, he wore a false nose made of silver.

Sneeze explosion

Itchiness inside the nose can trigger
a sneeze – a reflex action that removes
irritation by forcing air through
the nasal cavity and out the nostrils.
Thousands of droplets can be blasted
out with every sneeze, and may spread
cold or flu germs to other people.

Auditory canal

Leading to the ear from its
opening in the upper throat, the
auditory canal keeps air pressure
inside the ear the same as outside.
If the pressure is different, as it is
when a plane takes off, hearing
becomes difficult. A yawn will
open up the tube, make the ears
"pop", and restore normal hearing.

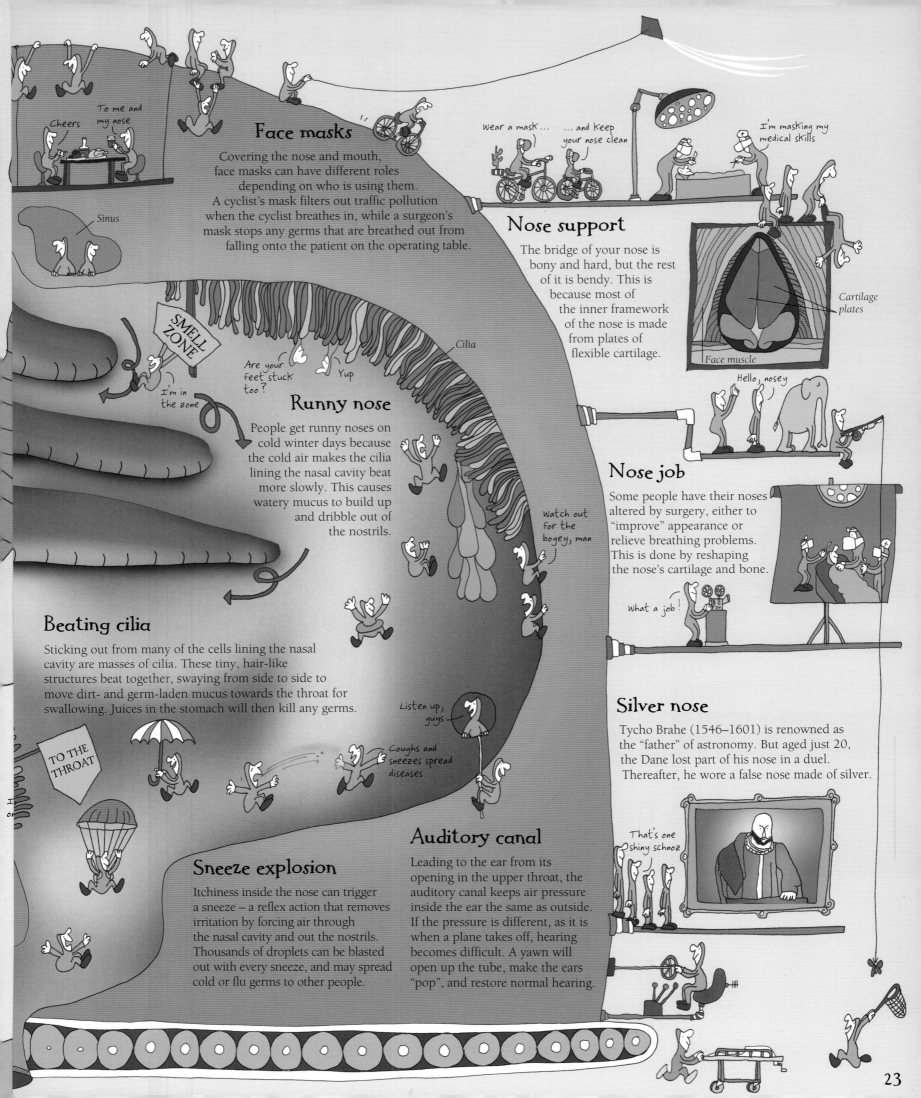

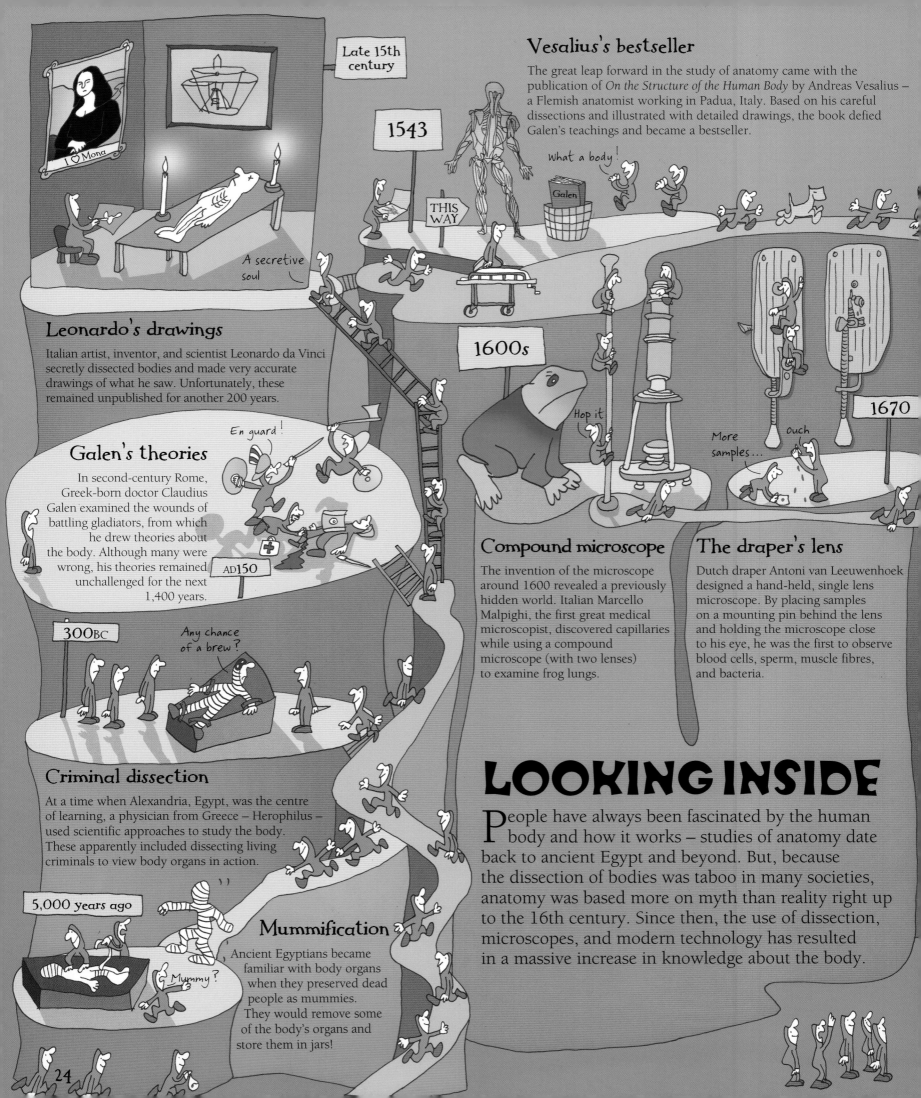

Vesalius's bestseller

The great leap forward in the study of anatomy came with the publication of *On the Structure of the Human Body* by Andreas Vesalius – a Flemish anatomist working in Padua, Italy. Based on his careful dissections and illustrated with detailed drawings, the book defied Galen's teachings and became a bestseller.

Late 15th century

1543

THIS WAY

A secretive soul

What a body!

Galen

I ♡ Mona

Leonardo's drawings

Italian artist, inventor, and scientist Leonardo da Vinci secretly dissected bodies and made very accurate drawings of what he saw. Unfortunately, these remained unpublished for another 200 years.

1600s

Hop it

1670

More samples...

Ouch

Galen's theories

In second-century Rome, Greek-born doctor Claudius Galen examined the wounds of battling gladiators, from which he drew theories about the body. Although many were wrong, his theories remained unchallenged for the next 1,400 years.

En guard!

AD150

Compound microscope

The invention of the microscope around 1600 revealed a previously hidden world. Italian Marcello Malpighi, the first great medical microscopist, discovered capillaries while using a compound microscope (with two lenses) to examine frog lungs.

The draper's lens

Dutch draper Antoni van Leeuwenhoek designed a hand-held, single lens microscope. By placing samples on a mounting pin behind the lens and holding the microscope close to his eye, he was the first to observe blood cells, sperm, muscle fibres, and bacteria.

300BC

Any chance of a brew?

Criminal dissection

At a time when Alexandria, Egypt, was the centre of learning, a physician from Greece – Herophilus – used scientific approaches to study the body. These apparently included dissecting living criminals to view body organs in action.

5,000 years ago

Mummy?

Mummification

Ancient Egyptians became familiar with body organs when they preserved dead people as mummies. They would remove some of the body's organs and store them in jars!

LOOKING INSIDE

People have always been fascinated by the human body and how it works – studies of anatomy date back to ancient Egypt and beyond. But, because the dissection of bodies was taboo in many societies, anatomy was based more on myth than reality right up to the 16th century. Since then, the use of dissection, microscopes, and modern technology has resulted in a massive increase in knowledge about the body.